Hannah and Hanna

A play

John Retallack

Samuel French — London

Hannah and Hanna was first published
in the volume *The Drama Book*
(English and Media Centre, 2002)

HANNAH AND HANNA

First presented by the Channel Theatre Company in Margate on the 20th June 2001, with the following cast:

Hannah	Alyson Coote
Hanna	Celia Meiras

Directed by John Retallack
Designed by Phil Newman
Choreographed by Andy Howitt
Music arranged by Karl James
Lighting designed by Nicci Spalding

CHARACTERS

Hannah: English; 16
Hanna (Xhevahinja): ethnic Albanian asylum-seeker from Kosovo; 16

Other characters played by **Hannah**:

Joe: Hannah's brother, a new policeman; 22
Nan: Hannah's grandmother; 75
Bullfrog: Hannah's bloke, unemployed; 18

Other characters played by **Hanna**:

Albin: Hanna's brother, an engineering student; 19
Flora: Hanna's mother, a recent widow, a doctor in Kosovo; 38
Bullfrog: Hannah's bloke, unemployed; 18

The action of the play is set in Margate and Kosovo

Time — summer 1999 to spring 2000

AUTHOR'S NOTE

Hannah and Hanna is a play for two young actors. It is about English teenagers finding the arrival of asylum-seekers in their area very hard to handle. Of course, stories around this theme are normally the other way about. It is the journey of the refugee that is the stuff of drama. I want to look at the situation another way. I want to acknowledge the role of us, the English audience, in the drama. "We" are the hosts who determine the fate of such people, our guests. "We" are thus central characters, rather than onlookers and outsiders. To the asylum-seekers, "we" are certainly the main players. There are some wonderfully inspiring accounts of English people who have acted magnanimously. There are many more accounts of English people who have not.

My play begins with a young English girl, still at school, who is the child of such people. Drama requires conflict, and, for a young English audience, this is where the story of the asylum-seekers begins — in their home town and in conflict.

That's why I want to start with teenagers. They mimic the attitudes of their parents, yet, unlike their parents, they can change their minds. If they can change their minds, they can still change the world. I read that the build-up of peoples wandering the world without a country to return home to (because of flood, famine or war) will increase many many times over in the course of the next five to ten years. It's the dull and cursing hosts — and, most of all, their children — that hold the destiny of these peoples in their hands.

John Retallack

HANNAH AND HANNA: PERFORMANCE HISTORY

Hannah and Hanna was first performed at the Channel Theatre Company Studio on June 21, 2001 by Alyson Coote as Margate Hannah and Celia Meiras as Kosovan Hanna.

This cast performed the play over a hundred times at several venues – the Gilded Balloon in Edinburgh for a month, the Arcola Theatre in London for a month and at BAC for three weeks. They also toured London schools (with an award from the Network for Social Change) for a further three weeks.

The play won a Glasgow Herald Angel at the Edinburgh Fringe, was part of the Time Out Critics Choice festival, was nominated as Best Young People's Show at the TMA awards and also for Race in the Media Award as a result of its broadcast on the World Service in June 2002.

In 2002, UK Arts International produced the play and toured it nationally with a new cast; Jenny Platt as Margate Hannah and Erin Brodie as Kosovan Hanna.

In 2003 and 2004, UK Arts International sent the play on two further extensive national tours with Louise Fitzgerald as Margate Hannah and Beth Cooper as Kosovan Hanna.

During this period the play also toured India (2003)), The Philippines (2004) and Malaysia (2005) for the British Council.

Hannah and Hanna has been translated and performed in Hebrew, Swedish and French (published in Editions La Fontaine, Lille, November 2004), and will be staged in Portuguese in 2005 and in Italian and in Dutch in 2006.

The play was revived for its third season at Theatre de Poche in Brussels in January 2005. A French tour is planned in spring 2005.

Hannah and Hanna is the first production of *Company of Angels* (www.companyofangels.co.uk) and was made possible by a Making Art Matter award from Arts Council (South East) and further grants from the Esmee Fairbairn Foundation, Lloyds TSB and Awards For All. The play was a co-production with Channel Theatre Company.

ACT I
Scene 1

Margate. Summer 1999

The floor of the stage is painted to represent the wooden planking of a seaside pier. US is a picture signifying Margate, displayed in such a way that other pictures can be easily substituted for it as the play proceeds. Below the picture is a narrow ledge at sitting height. There are two wooden boxes on stage, each about the size of an average suitcase; when the play begins these are side by side US, forming a platform. An operational karaoke machine with the name Hannah on it in large capitals stands on the platform. To either side of the stage are two screens, behind which are the props that Hannah and Hanna bring on to the stage, each of them having their own nominated screen and not using the other. Across the front of the stage (and up the sides if a thrust stage is being used) are pier railings; two identical baseball caps hang on these

The Lights come up

Hannah and Hanna enter from opposite sides of the stage. Hannah is English, brassily made up, with her hair up; Hanna, Kosovan, is plainly dressed and wears no make-up. Each has photographs that they show the audience in turn during the following

Hannah That's Margate from my window.
Hanna That's Pristina, from the window of my old house.
  Pristina is the capital city of Kosovo.
Hannah That's me on the beach.
  You can't see me because it's packed.
Hanna That's me in a truck on its way from Kosovo to Dover.
  You can't see me because I am hiding in the truck.
Hannah That's the block of flats I live in with my nan.
Hanna That's the window of the room which I share with my mother and
  my brother in the Hotel Bellevue in Margate.
Hannah That's my brother Joe.
  He's twenty-two and already a policeman.
  Ugly, ain't he?

Hanna   This is my mother.
              She sits all day looking at the sea from our window.

Hannah   And that's my bloke; everyone calls him Bullfrog —
              Well, Bull to his face.

Hanna   And this is my brother Albin.
              He walks around all day with the other young Kosovan guys.
              They have nothing to do.
              Handsome, isn't he?

Hannah   My name is Hannah.
              I'm sixteen.
              I've lived in Margate all my life.
              Margate — what a town!
              I hate it!

Hanna   My name is Hanna.
              I'm sixteen.
              I've lived in Margate for three days.
              Margate — what a town!
              I love it!

Hannah   Summer in Margate.
              July was crap.
              August is scorching hot.

Hanna   This is my new home.
              I fear nothing.

Hannah   The beaches are full of bodies.
              So are the hotels, four or five to a room.

Hanna   Only thing I fear is leaving Margate.
              Going home.

Hannah   But it's not like the old days.
              The people on the beaches ain't the same as the people in the
                  hotels.

Hanna   Three months of hiding in the mountains.
              Three days in a lorry to England.
              It is so nice to sleep in a bed.

Hannah   Bullfrog says "It's a bloody invasion,
              Kosovo arrived here in the night!"
              That pretty much sums up the feeling locally.

Hanna   My family lost everything.
              Except our freedom.
              When we arrived in Dover I kissed the ground.
              Free.
              At last.

Hannah sets up the karaoke machine during the following

Hanna moves away — either staying on stage or moving down into the audience

Hannah   Picture this:
I'm down on the seafront
With Bull and all his mates,
Doing what I do best
On a hot summer night.

SCENE 2

The Lights change to a setting evoking the seafront by night

With some ad-lib patter Hannah introduces "I Should Be So Lucky" by Kylie Minogue. She switches on the machine and sings the song to a backing tape. All the style and gesture is precisely reproduced. Hannah ad-libs so the audience sees she is performing for an onstage "audience" with whom she interacts either to insult (in reaction to their taunts) or flirt or show off

Hanna moves towards Hannah, watching her performance. Hannah spots Hanna and continues to sing. Then she stops singing, with the tape still playing and herself still moving to the music

Hannah   Are you another one of them?

Hanna is blank

Thought you were somehow, something in the air ... (*She sniffs*)
What can it be?
It's a sort of foreign smell — maybe it ain't you.
It must be the scum that comes in with the tide at night.
(*She sings again, then breaks off*)
You still standing there?
Where you from then?
Outer Mongolia?

Hanna is blank

Timbukbloodytoo?

Hanna is blank

(*Switching off the tape*) Don't tell me. I spy with my little eye someone beginning with "K".

Hannah reacts as if she has got a laugh from the "audience" for this. Hanna is still blank

> K-K-K-Kosovo … ?

Hanna looks down as if ashamed

> Haven't you got a tongue in your head?

Hannah takes in her friends laughing at Hanna. Hanna is silent

> Well, come on then Kosovan Spice, say something or die …

Hanna is silent. Hannah walks over to her and puts the microphone to Hanna's mouth

> OK, what's your name?

Hanna   My name is Hanna.

Hannah (*to Bull and her mates and the audience*) That ain't her real name.
They're all bloody liars.
Don't you know that much?
Yeah, it's so funny …
Oh, you can all sod off.

Hannah goes behind her screen with a clatter, taking her karaoke machine with her and leaving her friends behind

Hanna   My real name is Xhevahinja (*Jerve-a-heera*)
But no-one can pronounce it here.
My middle name is Hanna,
So here in Margate my mother named me again.
Hanna — because of all our sorrow,
And because it would help me to make friends in England.
I didn't mean to take her name.

SCENE 3

The Lights change to a different outdoor setting

Hannah comes out from behind her screen

Hannah   Cliftonville is a mile up from Margate.
It's all posh hotels and lawns
Looking over the sea.
There's a bowling green there

Where Bull and I always go
When it's hot and it's dark.
But I just wasn't in the mood ...
I was bloody furious, wouldn't you be?
It's *my* name and I ain't sharing it with an asylum-seeker!
Suddenly Bull's off on one ——

(*As Bull*) Bloody Kosovans.
Come over to Dover.
Nick yer house, your car, your girlfriend,
Load their trolleys up for nothing
And get a hundred pound a week —
For what? To have a lovely seaside holiday — for a year!
We should be so lucky.
That Kosovitch!
I'd tell her straight —
Go back home —
'N' give her a slap next time.

(*As Hannah*) That's my boy!
I'm the only Hannah round here aren't I?
(*She reacts as if Bull is walking towards h*er)
Come here, Bull. Where would I be without you?

Hannah returns behind her screen

Hanna   I go home and I am upset because the English don't like me.
Mother is crying in our room.
The sun is shining and she's crying.
My brother won't stay in our room.
He does not like her crying.
He goes out on the street all the day.
He walks in a gang to be safe.
Kosovan gang — English gang— very bad.
I don't like this English girl
But I like how she sings.
(*Pause*)
I sing too.
I know all the songs as well as her.
Everyone in Pristina knows English music.
I like Britney Spears, All Saints, Westlife, Celine Dion, Steps.

*Hanna sings "Tragedy" by Steps for a full minute, voice and gesture perfect,
with no accompaniment*

Some people here are stupid.
They don't like us here but they don't know us;
But Joe the policeman who protects our hotel,
He is smiling and makes jokes.
He makes us feel safe.
I am going to make the shopping
In Aldi's.

Hanna goes behind her screen

Hannah comes out from behind her screen wearing an Aldi's overall. She sets up the counter at Aldi's supermarket by moving the two boxes and turning them on to their ends. She stands behind the counter; till operations etc. are mimed

The Lights change to an indoor setting

Hannah   Aldi's: it's where I work on Saturday and Thursday nights.
Everyone goes there.
It's the cheapest shop in Margate.
Last Thursday, I'm standing here behind the counter,
There's a massive queue —
It's one of our busiest nights.

Hanna comes out from behind her screen wearing a cheap anorak and carrying a supermarket basket and shopping voucher. She stands as if queuing

And guess who is holding everyone up?
(*To Hanna*) Got an Aldi's card?
Hanna   No.
Hannah   Cashback?
Hanna   No. (*She holds out the voucher*)
Hannah   (*peering at Hanna's basket*) You can only spend ten pounds with
one of these you know.
You can't buy the whole shop.
Hanna   I have vouchers for myself, my brother and my mother.
That's thirty pounds.
Hannah   Your mother and brother here are they?
Hanna   No, they are at home.
Hannah   Where's that, then?
Hanna   Here, in Margate. I live here, you know.
Hannah   I thought your home was in Kosovo.
Margate's my home, not yours.

	You people just don't seem to realize that,
	However many times you're told it,
	Do you?
Hanna	I came here to buy food, not listen again to you.
	Please stop your talking.
Hannah	One voucher buys ten pounds of shopping,
	No change.
	One person one voucher per week.
	You'll have to put it back
	Or bring the rest of the family in.
	Call them on your mobile.
Hanna	I have not got a mobile.
Hannah	You've all got mobiles.
Hanna	I have no phone, I have no pounds.
	I take the bread, the butter, the jam, the apples, the oranges, the coffee, the sugar, the oil, the ham, the shampoo — seven pounds and five p; the banana, the washing powder, the aspirin, the Coke — nine pounds and fifty-seven p.
Hannah	No change.
Hanna	The baked beans.
Hannah	Nine pounds and eighty p,
	Get some matches and start a fire.
Hanna	You have the money,
	Why don't you set fire to yourself?

Hannah and Hanna walk DS *and face the audience. They are both very angry*

	She has no right to talk to me like that.
Hannah	You'd think she owned the bloody place the way she carries on.
Hanna	A lady in the queue said at least I stood up for myself.
Hannah	Next time I won't give her the chance.

They angrily knock over the boxes and exit

SCENE 4

The Lights change to a setting evoking the seafront by night

Hannah comes on with her karaoke machine and sets it up. She then repeats exactly the ad-lib patter she used to introduce the Kylie Minogue song in Scene 2 and sings "Baby One More Time" by Britney Spears with the karaoke machine to the same crowd that she did Kylie for

Hanna comes out from behind her screen and joins in, singing along really well and successfully for a sustained period until Hannah can stand it no longer and stops singing. The karaoke machine continues playing

Hannah   Shut up! I don't want to sing with you, talk to you
Or live in the same bloody town as you!
I don't want to breathe the same air as you people
So go away and stop stalking me round,
You freaky foreign person.
I don't want to see you again —
All right?

Hanna stares at Hannah

Don't stand there pretending you're a human.
You're Kosovan, that's a foreign word, means scum.

Hanna turns and very slowly returns behind the screen

(*Turning to her audience*) Well, what are you all staring at?
No surrender.
Like you said, ay, Bull?

Hannah sits down and stares, then goes behind her screen with the karaoke machine

Hanna comes out from behind her screen, running her fingers slowly along the railings

The Lights change to an indoor setting

Hannah brings out a chair and places it on stage during the following, returning behind her screen

Hanna   I am in England and I'm crying.
I tell my mother what happened;
She holds me in her arms
And then she makes me sit down and she talks to me.
She sits upright in her chair, like this.
(*In the course of the following she "becomes" her mother and sits in the chair*)
It's very hot so she's fanning herself.
The manager still hasn't fixed the window.
She talks to me a bit like a doctor talking to a patient.

That's what she is in Pristina, a doctor.
This is what she says to me, in our language — in Albanian.

(*As her mother*) As you know, your father loved the English
    language,
But most of all he loved the English people.
English was his life and his work;
He taught the language very well
And after the Serbs sacked him
He had only one student left —
You, his darling girl.
But there is one thing you must not forget:
Your father could talk all day about England —
Westminster, Brighton Pier, FA Cup, Tony Blair —
But he never came to England.
He never left Kosovo!
Unlike you, he never saw the sea,
Only mountains.
You know what I'm saying, don't you?
Kosovo was invaded and crushed for ten years.
He would say "The *English* would never let this happen to
    England!"
Your father imagined the English to be so good,
So honourable, so courageous, so decent.
Well, of course —
There never was a people like that anywhere …
I don't like the English who call us names
And if you father was alive and in Margate,
Neither would he.

(*As herself*) It's no use listening to my mother.
She thinks in Kosovan.
What am I supposed to do?
Stay in all day?

*Hanna goes behind her screen, taking the chair. During the following, she
returns with a different chair for Hannah's nan, then goes behind her screen
again*

*Hannah comes out with a laundry bag, a pile of library books and a
newspaper*

The Lights change to a different indoor setting

Hannah   I go home.
I'm churned up.
Just who does she think she is?
I've never been as hard as that before on anyone …
I had this sickly feeling in my gut …
(*She acts out the following*)
I stop on the way at the library and get Nan's books.
Nan's who I live with because me mum ain't around.
I pick up the washing from the launderette.
Almost forget her paper.
Climb eleven floors with the washing and the books,
'Cos the lift still ain't fixed.

(*As herself; to Nan*) Hallo, Nan.

(*Imagining Nan's reply*) Course it's me — who else is it gonna
be?

(*As herself; to the audience*) Nan's sitting in the corner of the
room.
Curtains drawn as usual.
The room smells of — I dunno —
But it smells.
I give her her paper.

(*To Nan*) Nan, you've got to start going out again;
It's beautiful outside.
You look like a ghost.

(*To the audience*) Tell you the truth
I can't stand being in the place with her.
But Joe's busy and if I don't do the necessaries
She'd fade away in her chair.
All you'd see is the *Margate Gazette*.
Muggers, drivers, robbers, pram-pushers 'n' dogwalkers —
She's afraid of them all.

(*As Nan*) Hannah!
They've put my letter in the paper.
The one about the pensioners.
The *Margate Gazette* is a good paper, you know.
They've put my letter near the top
By a picture of the Home Secretary.
"Is he listening to Margate?" it says.

(*As herself; to Nan*) Yeah, lovely, Nan.
But don't you think it's more important that you go out?

(*To the audience*) She's about to lecture me about why she lives
    indoors all the time
But instead my brother Joe makes a visit
Looking very smart in his uniform.
As usual, he says:

(*As Joe*) Don't go up to Cliftonville tonight, Hannah, I'm telling
    you.
There'll be trouble and I don't want you involved —
Right?

(*As herself*) Right you are, Joe, never trust me, do you?

She moves Nan's chair to one side

(*To the audience*) Course I'll be there.

Fatboy Slim's "Right Here Right Now" plays under the following

It's Saturday night.
Keep me head low from Joe —
He can smell smoke on me breath at fifty paces.
In this town trouble's a magnet.
What else is there to look for in Margate?
It's a year-round rumble for having to live in the place —
And now we can hit Kosovans
'Stead of each other.
I wanna go there.
So I'll end up there,
Joe or no Joe —
Magnetic, see?

The volume of the music rises

*Hanna comes on; she and Hannah perform a choreographed dance sequence
representing a street fight. The music ends*

SCENE 5

The Lights change to an outdoor setting

Hanna   Saturday night in Cliftonville.

Hannah   Same street.
Hanna   Same wall.
Hannah   Same aggro bubbling under.
              Bull's there. Finished work at six,
              Had four pints by eight.
              It's a hot night;
              He's in shorts, shades,
              And a shirt with "Kosoville" on it in letters of dripping blood.
Hanna   Albin and his friends are bored of being told to go home.
              They decide to walk across the road,
              Play a football game.
Hannah   Nine-a-side,
              Shirts for goal posts;
              Stripped to the waist 'n' off they go.
              Kosovan asylum-seeker team A versus Kosovan asylum-seeker
                  team B.
Hanna   The Kosovans play football very good.
              All the girls see that, so the boys do too, I know.
Hannah   Nothing happens, we're quite happy to watch the game.
              Then whose idea is it to nick the bloody ball?
Hanna   Her stupid ugly boyfriend runs on to the grass,
              Puts the ball under his arm and runs towards the cliff.
Hannah   Off goes Bull followed by eighteen Kosovan lads,
              Each one bare-chested and with a knife in his pocket,
              Screaming blue murder, in Albanian,
              Chased by another thirty Margate kids;
              Then two coppers, screaming into the radiophones for help …
Hanna   Ugly boy reaches the clifftop,
              Kicks the ball up into the air,
              Down into the sea below.
Hannah   Hang on, the ball goes up into the air
              But not down into the sea.
              It hovers,
              Seems to stop and have a think,
              Changes its mind
              And falls on to the tarmac into the middle of fifty panting youths.
Hanna   Albin jumps up and catches it
              And off he goes running like the wind,
              Back over the grass,
              Across the road
              Down Ethelred Crescent —
              Fifty of us chasing the ball in Albin's hands —
              Why?

	I don't *know* why
	But I can't stop running …
Hannah	Bull's running across the tops of cars —
	His favourite trick.
	The dog-walkers and pram-pushers dive for cover
	And a lady with a stick goes flying across the pavement.
	Someone screams and there's a crash of glass.
	On we go,
	Into the road;
	Cars screech out the way.
Hanna **Hannah**	(*together*) CRASH!
Hanna	The car hits the lamppost and stops,
	The post like this. (*She demonstrates a bent post*)
	I don't stop,
	I don't care, I just run and run,
	Faster now,
	Down the hill;
	There's more than fifty of us now.
Hannah	A bus swerves;
	It nearly, oh-so-nearly, goes flat upon its side.
	You should have heard the screams inside.
	Loud enough to wake the dead of Margate.
Hanna	We turn a corner and I see the beach, the bay, the lights.
	Many, many people too.
	For one second I see Albin
	Still in front, his face a knife;
	Then on he goes, he's gone.
Hannah	I turn round for a second,
	Look behind;
	In the dying light I see 'bout eighty of 'em
	And I'm telling you
	For one second I thought:
	"If the Kosovans need Margate,
	Then Margate needs the Kosovans!
	When last did we have such a time as *this?*"
Hanna	Faster and faster
	Down the hill to the beach. I can't stop running.
	My legs are moving faster;
	I can't stop my legs.
	On to the sand.
Hannah	We hit the beach.
	The Kosovan with the ball stops.

Hanna   Albin kicks it in the air
Hannah   It lands in the sea and bobs about on the tide.
Hanna   The stupidest fight you've ever seen begins.
Hannah ⎫
Hanna ⎭ (*together*) All in slow motion.
Hannah   The breath has gone from everybody
              The sand soaks up the action.

They flop

Hanna   (*her hands on her knees, breathing heavily; alert*)
              Ugly boy is moving through the gasping bodies.
              He's moving towards Albin.
              Albin doesn't see him.
Hannah   I look up to see Bull land a heavy punch
              To the head of the Kosovan who carried the ball.
Hannah   He drops like a stone.
              Everyone around Bull's cheering.
              Bull's goin' mad.
Hanna   He's kicking Albin in the head.
              Albin!
Hannah   Bull! What d' ya think you're doing!
Hanna   (*screaming*) Albin!
Hannah   (*screaming*) Bull!

They both run towards Bull and mime attempting to pull him off Albin

Hanna ⎫
Hannah ⎭ (*together*)Get off get off get off!

Hannah turns and reacts as if seeing her brother

Hanna "sees" the policeman who visited her hotel

Hanna   Look, it's the policeman from our hotel …
              Look! Look!
Hannah   Joe! Joe! Pull him off before he kills him!

They mime pulling Bull off Albin, their actions stylized and identical

Hannah   Joe had him in an arm-lock and out of view in seconds flat. I saw
              him and a woman copper take him off.
Hanna   Albin was still bleeding from his nose and head. (*She turns to
              address Hannah*) Please … Hannah …

Hannah turns reluctantly to Hanna

         Please help me lift him up.
         I have to take him home.
Hannah   You'll never get him back up to Cliftonville.
         We've just run a mile and a half downhill.
         Just wait for an ambulance.
Hanna   If they think he's making all this trouble
         They put him in prison till he goes back to Kosovo.
         Please please help.
         It's your boyfriend who beat him.
Hannah (*to the audience*) There was fighting all around us and screaming.
         Her brother started groaning.
         I said
         (*To Hanna*) OK. My flat's crap but it's near the beach. Come with
         me.
Hanna   I will. Thank you Hannah.
Hannah (*to the audience*) Sometimes you just have to grit your teeth, don't
         you?

SCENE 6

Groove Armada's "By the River" plays

The Lights change to a different outdoor setting

Hanna takes a bandanna from her pocket and ties it round her head to become Albin

Hannah carries Hanna/Albin around the stage and on to one of the boxes (representing the tower block). Hannah mimes pressing the bell of the intercom

Hannah (*to Nan; into the intercom*)
         Hi, Nan, it's me.
         No, I've got my key.
         I'm just bringing two visitors up, OK?
         No, you don't know them.
         One of them's hurt, OK?
         Is the lift … ?
         Good!
         (*To the audience*)
         We put him in the lift; I was shaking.

The Lights change to an indoor setting. Hannah and Hanna step down from the box. Nan's chair is moved C

> We get to my door.
> Nan's standing there.
> She screams her head off.
> I ain't ever heard her scream before.
> Goes to her room
> And slams the door.

The music ends

Hanna (*to the audience*) We made Albin comfortable.
> Then we saw each other. We were both covered in blood.
> (*To Hannah*) Keep him awake.
> I won't be long.
Hannah (*to Hanna*) Where are you going?
Hanna   To get my mother. She knows what to do.
Hannah You can't leave me here …

Hanna goes behind her screen

> (*To the audience*) The front door slams.
> She's gone.
> Nan's door opens.
> Her head peeps round.
>
> (*As Nan*) Have they gone?
>
> (*As herself*) — she says.
> Out she comes,
> Slap into Albin
> Bleeding over her favourite chair.
> I almost died.
> She didn't move or say nothing.
> Then,
>
> (*As Nan*) We better clean the poor sod up, hadn't we?
> His mother can't see him like this.
>
> (*As herself*) And she takes over, fussing over Albin — he was
>   Albin now —
> Like he was her own.
> She dabbed and wiped.
> Albin groaned in pain.
> Then the buzzer went.

Hanna comes out as her mother, no longer wearing the bandanna and carrying a handbag

Hanna (*to the audience*) My mother walks in.
Hannah   She's not what I expected;
No headscarf, no anorak.
She smells of nice perfume.
She's quite a lady.
She checks over Albin — very professional —
Then gives him a *big* cuddle.
She smiles at Nan, who almost curtsies;
Then Hanna's mother tries to thank my nan.
Hanna (*as her Mother: to Nan*) You — very — good — English — dame.
Hannah   Before
Nan thought Kosovans were all a bunch of hooligans.

(*As Nan to Mother*) Your English ain't up to much is it, love?

(*To the audience*) She's very impressed.
Offers her a cup of tea.
Hanna (*as her Mother*) Thank you, madam.
Hannah   Then Joe turns up and is about to start on me.
Nan cuts in, quite posh.
"Don't start now, Joe,
We've got some visitors from abroad."
Hanna (*to the audience*) We see the figure of a policeman at the door.
The asylum-seekers turn to stone.
We feel guilty.
It's automatic.
So crazy.
Hanna's grandmother introduces him as Joe, her grandson.
It's him.
The policeman from our hotel.
The policeman on the beach.
The angel policeman.
Albin nods to him, very polite.
Mother shakes his hand.
I stand staring like I do.
Hannah   I'm getting this sickly feeling in my gut again.
I feel dizzy.
Hanna   I'm glad to be here.
Everyone safe.
Albin is on his feet.

	Mother smiling.
	And I've found Hannah.
	Without even looking for her.
	She's standing by the doorway now —
	I can't see her face ...
Hannah	I watch them sitting, three Kosovans,
	An angry pensioner and a policeman ...
	Why can't I let go and enjoy the party too?
Hanna	I translate for Albin and for my mother.
	Her name is Flora which makes them laugh
	Because in England it means margarine.
	Hannah's grandmother asked us if we will come back next Friday
	And of course my mother says we will.
	This is the first time my mother has left the hotel
	Since we arrived.
	The first time she has used
	The English that she knows.
	Albin doesn't speak
	But I know he understands.
	He is quiet with the policeman.
	It was Albin who had the ball.
	After some time we say goodbye and thank you.
	Many times.
	Hannah comes out of the shadow.
	(*To Hannah*) Do you mind if I come and see you again?
Hannah	Yeah,
	We'll do a song or something in my room, OK?
Hanna	Thank you, Hannah.
Hannah	(*to the audience*) Go on, hate me, I do.
	I just wanted to do something,
	Something nice like everyone else seemed to be doing.
	And it made my stomach feel better,
	So it was the right thing
	For me to do
	At the time.
	Right?

"Torn" by Natalie Imbruglia plays over the theatre speakers. Hannah and Hanna sing to the CD. This is a turning point for them; they take some time to thaw out and though the singing is good, it takes until the end of the song for the girls to be at ease with each other

Hanna	What do you want to be when you grow up?

Hannah I wanna be rich.
            What do you want to be?
Hanna   I want to be a pharmacist.

The music fades

Hannah (*to the audience*) All this leaves out Bullfrog.
            I couldn't tell him about Hanna and me.
            He'd turn into a one-man mental institution.
            I liked him.
            Till that night on the beach
            When he tasted blood.
            Once Hanna walked past me and Bull on the front
            And I had to do it.
            I had to pretend I was the same as I was before.
            (*Shouting directly at Hanna*)
            Kosovo. Scum. Go home.

Hannah and Hanna both turn to face the audience

            I'm so sorry.
            I had to do that.
            I'm so sorry, Hanna.
Hanna   It's OK. In my country it happens all the time.

Hannah and Hanna move to opposite sides of the stage

Hannah Things have changed.
            Me and Hanna are like Nan now.
Hanna   Like Nan *was.*
Hannah Oh yeah.
            She goes out now.
            All by herself.
Hanna   My mum and Albin and Joe all meet for tea on Fridays.
Hannah My nan's started the Kosovan branch of the Women's
              Institute ...
            If Bull finds out
            I'll be the one needing asylum.
Hanna   (*of Hannah*) She worries too much.
            I love being in her flat.
            Eleven floors up looking over the sea.
            We are singing every day.
            No-one can see us.
            No-one can hear us.

Hannah and Hanna change their positions to indicate a passage of time

Hannah   It was getting boring, staying in.
             So we went out,
             Sang on the front.
             Bull was there.
             But I weren't bothered.
             We just sung
             Our favourite song.

Hannah urges the anxious Hanna on to the box platform. They sing and dance a perfected, unaccompanied version of "Perfect" by Fairground Attraction. This is a real performance piece the girls have worked on for weeks

Hannah and Hanna become Bull, taking the caps from the railing, putting them on and speaking in unison to the audience

Hannah } *(together; as Bull)* Gotcha!
Hanna   } Asylum lover.
               Kosovo lesbo.
               Margate bloody traitor.
               English scum.
               You come out on the front again,
               You're dead.
               Hear that,
               You're dead.
               Hannah,
               Bloody Hannah:
               Dead,
               Right?
               Dead.

Hannah and Hanna exit separately

ACT II

SCENE 1

The Margate picture US *has been replaced by one depicting a grey sea with seagulls. The railings and the chairs have been removed. The boxes are on their sides with a gap between them; the props for Act II are brought from the boxes rather than from behind the screens*

When Act II begins, Hannah — now in drab clothes, with no make-up and her hair down — and Hanna are on stage in darkness. The Lights come up on them

Hannah (*to the audience*) One night, just before Christmas,
    Bull and his mates — his "bully-boys" as he likes to call 'em —
    They ambushed us as we came out the main door of the flats.
    It was me they wanted to hurt, not Hanna.

A piano version of "Good King Wenceslas" plays. In a choreographed sequence, Hannah is spat at, kicked and trodden on by Hanna as Bull. The music ends

During the following scene, each keeps to her side of the stage as they are in separate rooms

Hanna (*as herself; to the audience*) I sit in the library because it is warm and
    I read English books.
    We don't meet any more, not even in secret.
    Hannah is hurt.
    She is afraid of Bull now.
    I know very well how she is feeling
    But I miss her.
    I haven't seen her for days.
Hannah I've stopped going out just for the time being.
    It's pretty horrible out there anyway.
    Joe keeps an eye on our door, which is nice.
    When the lift broke again I asked Joe not to get it fixed.
    I feel safer up here that way.
    Anyway, whenever I bin out lately I was getting "English scum,
      asylum-lover",
    All that crap in my ears.

And it weren't just me: Joe got it too.
Once word got out about Nan's Friday tea-parties.
He had the piss taken once too often.
Joe ended up in a fight himself over it.
Nan didn't like both of us getting grief;
So she closed down the tea-parties.
Now Nan moans at *me* for never going out.
But she looks after me
Like I looked after her.
When the rain beats on the windows all through the afternoon
All I can see is grey shite and seagulls.

A piano version of Nina Simone's "Little Girl Blue" plays

I've started going through my mum's old vinyls.
It cheers me up.
Nan says my mum was a bit of a singer,
Into all kinds of music.
Folk, jazz, you name it.
I never listened to it before.
Some of the stuff in here is all right.
I learn the ones I really like,
Put them on a tape.
Nan delivers the tape — plus my letter — to Hanna,
Then Nan stops and talks to Flora for about nine hours.
Gawd knows what they got to talk about
Considering they hardly understand one another.
By the time she leaves
Hanna's already written me her letter back.

Hanna I am learning the new songs in bed, sometimes in the dark.
The manager says there are too many heaters in the hotel;
If you turn one on, all the lights go off,
So it's cold and that's why I am in bed.

Hannah and Hanna collect Walkman headphones from the boxes and put them on. They sing "Little Girl Blue" as if they are singing along to a tape. The music ends

Hannah sits on her box, staring DS as if through a window, then takes a letter from the box and opens it. She reads it and acts it out as Hanna recites it

Mother stays in all day now.
I cannot make her go out.
She cannot work here even though she is a children's doctor.
Mother and Albin get more and more sad together.

I listen to your tape and I can't hear them talking,
When the weather is very bad,
I take the Walkman to the beach.
With the rain in my face
I forget everyone and everything.
I try and see you at your window
But it's too far away.
Maybe you can see me.
When I get in from the storm outside
The room feels warmer.
Mother and Albin are sleeping.
They sleep hours every day.
Dreaming of leaving,
Dreaming of home.
Happy Millennium, Hannah.

They sing part of Abba's "Mamma Mia" without accompaniment and with headphones, each in their own world

Hannah takes a 2000 hairband out of her box, puts it on and again stares DS as if out of the window. Hanna takes a party popper from her box and lets it off, then produces and opens a letter. She reads the letter as Hannah recites it

Hannah   Happy Millennium, Hanna!
Bull is sending nasty stuff in the mail.
Really evil stuff, some of it.
I don't know what's happened to his sense of humour.
He's obsessed.
And since things are quieter at your hotel,
Joe spends more time keeping an eye on my door
Than he does on yours.
Bull seems to think I'm the asylum-seeker now
So it's me who gets the treatment
'Cos I don't hate you.
He hates me.
It's stupid and it's doing my bloody head in.
Every time I think I'll go out,
I wanna be sick
But I'll keep writing
And sending you the tapes, just for now.
Joe got into trouble for that scrap I told you about.
Nearly lost his job.

Coppers can't get into punch-ups.
It's illegal.
He's going to do something about it, he says,
But he won't say what.

(*As Joe*) You'll see ——

(*As herself*) — he says ——

(*As Joe*) — you'll see.

(*As herself*) The longer I stay in
The harder it is to go out ...
I'll come and see you soon.
Promise.
PS: Do you like that song by the A-Teens?
I hope you like it as much as I do.

The A-Teens' "Mamma Mia" plays at a low volume. Hannah and Hanna make a series of tableaux to show the months passing

Hannah ⎫
Hanna ⎬ (*together*) January. February. March. April.

The music increases in volume. They dance to "Mamma Mia", each still in their own separate room, with great emotion, Hanna liberated, Hannah raging. The music volume drops. Hannah opens a letter that Hanna speaks as "Mamma Mia" continues underneath

Hanna   I have big news!
Joe is driving a lorry to Pristina.
He is taking medicines to hospitals
And as my mother is a doctor,
She may be allowed to go with him!
And Albin!
And *me*!
I don't want to go back to bloody Kosovo!
But nobody listens to me!
Hannah (*to the audience*) Nan always said,
Joe's a good deed.
And you're a bad deed.
Bloody Joe.
(*To Hanna*) Joe!

During the following, Hanna moves around the set as Joe, moving and fixing things as she speaks, getting ready for the journey

Hanna (*as Joe*)   What?
Hannah   You didn't tell me!
Hanna (*as Joe*)   What?
Hannah   This! (*She waves the letter*)
Hanna (*as Joe*)   Sorry ... I had to ask them first, didn't I?
Hannah   You can't leave me alone in Margate!
Hanna (*as Joe*)   People miss you, you know that?
Hannah   I don't miss them.
Hanna (*as Joe*)   You can't lock yourself up in here forever.
          You gotta face the world again, Hannah.

Hanna takes a letter from her box and gives it to Hannah; Hannah opens it

Hanna (*reciting the letter*) We are leaving next week.
          My mother is so happy she can't stop smiling.
          I want to see you to say goodbye.
Hannah   Thing is, somehow, we're best friends.
          Even though I never see Hanna
          I can't face not seeing her again.
Hanna   Can we meet by the clock-tower at twelve tomorrow?
Hannah (*to the audience*) I know it's stupid, but like my nan,
          I've built up this fear of going out.
          Of course, like her, I'll go out and I won't see what I fear;
          I won't see Bull or his mates.
          I'll just walk up to the clock-tower and we'll jump about
          And then we'll go up to the hotel together
          And I'll wave them off to Kosovo.
          Sad how I feel jealous of an asylum-seeker
          For leaving Margate ...
          I used to think they were lucky to be here.

Hannah exits

Hanna changes the picture back to Margate and moves both boxes to one side

The volume of the music comes up again for the finale

Hannah enters wearing a jacket and carrying a rucksack, looking fresh, herself again

I go out.
It's a hot spring day like you get now —
The sea and the sun hit me like I'm in Spain
Or some other place I've never been to.
I feel fabulous
Like Hanna said she felt when she got here last summer.
Nan has put some sandwiches in a bag
Like I'm going on a picnic and made me promise
I'll be home by four.
"Don't worry," I said, "I'll probably be home for lunch."
And eat them on the sofa.

(*As Nan*) You'll eat them alone ——

(*As herself*) — she said ——

(*As Nan*) — I'm out today.

(*As herself*) She's never in these days, my nan.
As I walk along the front I feel I'm flying.
Here I am, free again and newly born.
A second later I hear the chant I hate and fear:

Hanna ⎫
Hannah ⎭ (*together*) *Kosovans go home, go back home!* ——

Hannah — 'cept this time it isn't just Bull,
But what sounds like a pub full of monster blokes.
My stomach churns with fear.
I feel I'm being told to go back home.
Instantly, I want to run back to the flat.
I turn round and there they are,
The National Front in triumph straggling along Sea Road.
They've brought kiddies too — boy Nazis and toy Nazis,
Even a little pushchair Nazi crying his eyes out,
All bellowing down the front at no-one in particular,
Just a load of coppers and bored Margate people staring.
I'm standing there
Taking this in
And I hear ——

Hanna ⎫
Hannah ⎭ (*together*) *Out, out, out!* ——

Hannah — chanted from behind me.
Yes, it's the other mob, the Anti-Nazi League,
Coming towards me!

They're arm in arm, all shapes and sizes,
And in the front line —
My nan!
The Kosovans have turned my family inside out!
Joe going there today in a truck,
Nan fighting the National Front.
What have I been doing all winter?
I want to help Nan or save her or something.
But when I look at her
Her head held high and her looking so proud
I want to hide away again.
I turn and run.
In panic I slip,
Arse over tit in the path of the National Front,
And I'm looking up at Bull.
Ugly bastard in a T-shirt
With a union jack turned into a bloody swastika across the front,
Yelling:

Hanna ⎫ (*together, as Bull*) *England for the English!*
Hannah ⎭

(*As herself; to the audience*) A second later he'd see me.
This time I get in first.
(*She mimes kicking*)
Crunch!
He went:

(*As Bull*) *England for the — aargh!*

(*As herself; to the audience*) I heard but I didn't see.
I was gone.

Alice DJ's "Are You Better Off Alone?" plays loudly and continues quietly through the following

Hannah exits

Hanna takes a long-sleeved top from her box and ties it round her waist

Hanna(*jumping up and down as if by a lamppost, wanting to see and not be seen; to the audience*) It's twelve o' clock and there is a war starting around me.

This is the place we said we'd meet.
Hannah, hurry, please, hurry Hannah.

Hannah enters and runs past Hanna

Hannah!

The music surges

*The two girls dance and mime a long chase. During the chase they move the
boxes to form a lorry: one box is laid on its side* US *to form the back, the other
flat in front of it to form the cab; both are at an angle across the stage. Hannah
and Hanna also change the Margate picture to one showing complete
blackness*

The music finishes abruptly

Hannah hides behind the US *box. She is not seen by Hanna*

SCENE 2

Hanna (*to the audience*) I've lost her.
        She's not at the hotel.
        She's not by the lorry.
        Joe is shouting at me that we're leaving *now*.
        Mother and Albin are waving at me.
        The National Front are coming up the hill.
        I don't want to leave.
        I don't want to leave.

*The lighting changes; the front and the back portions of the lorry are
illuminated, with darkness between them*

*Hanna sits down in the front of the lorry. The lorry departs with both girls
aboard*

        We've left.
        We're going down the hill
        In a lorry with "Kosovo Aid" written along its side.
        Spit hits the window by my head.
        I look at the beach and sea for a last second.
        I'm looking everywhere for Hannah.
        We drive past the back of the sign that says

"Welcome to Margate".
She's gone.
I can't see her.
I've lost her.
Where was she running?
Why was she running from me?

Hannah (*emerging from behind the box; to the audience*) I can't see a thing
in here.
It's totally black.
I want to scream my bloody head off,
But then I'd give myself away.
No-one's going to find me here.
No-one.

Hanna Dover.
I remember Dover.
Three days and three nights in a lorry to get here.
We were hidden in the back all that time.
There were twelve of us and a baby.
The mother had put her hand over his mouth
Every time we stopped.
There was a hole in the top for light
A hole in the floor for toilet.
We paid three thousand pounds to come to Dover;
Everything that my father had left to us.
When the door opened on the third night
We put up our hands.
We thought we would be shot.
The man said, "Get out now" and we did;
Then he drove away.
I did not know what country we were standing in
Till I saw the sign for Dover.

Hannah I've been sleeping for hours.
I don't know what time it is.
I finished the sandwiches a long time ago.
I've kept the chocolate for emergency.
But I'm starving.
There's a plastic bin to pee in,
But no lid.
Nan will be home now.
She'll think I'm a dirty stop-out.

Hanna Calais, Dunkirk, Zeebrugge, Ghent,
Brussels, Aachen, Cologne, Frankfurt.
Albin is driving now.

Mother wants me to sing but I can't.
I left my voice in Margate.
Everything I want to forget
I remember like yesterday.
Nuremberg, Passau, Graz, Leibnitz …

Hannah sings a verse of Bob Dylan's "Shelter from the Storm" unaccompanied

Hannah (*speaking*) Chocolate's gone. I'm so hungry
So hungry.
So hungry.

Hanna sings the next verse

Hanna (*speaking*) Joe says, "My mother used to sing that! How do you
know it?"
I say:
When Hannah was alone in the flat
She learnt many old songs.
Your Nan brought them to me on cassettes
While Nan listened to Mother talking,
I learnt them.
If Hannah was here
We could sing a whole concert.
Mother says:

(*As her mother*) Your Nan helped me very much, Joe.
She made me talk of everything until I stopped crying.
That's why we're going home now.

(*As herself; to the audience*) Joe and Mother tell me to sing more.
I want to sleep.
I want to go backwards.
I want to wake up again in Dover.

They sing another verse and chorus of "Shelter from the Storm"

Hannah I'm turning into a cockroach in here,
A blind, dirty thing that lives in the dark.
I'm not coming out.
I'm not coming out.
They can lock me up or beat me up
But I'm going all the way.

Hanna   We stop, we start again, on and on and on.
We are always crossing borders.
I go to sleep in Hungary, wake in Romania ...
The lorry is moving but I am not moving.
I am sleeping in the Hotel Bellevue,
Dreaming we are driving,
Driving ... dreaming ...

(*As her mother*) Wake up, Hanna, wake up!

(*As herself*) My mother is shaking me.

Hanna wakes up, doesn't know what's happening, where she is

(*As her mother*) Look! Kosovo!

(*As herself*) I've been stuck so long in my seat
I don't know that we are moving.
I open the door to step out of the lorry
My mother grabs on to my coat.
I am falling out of my coat.
Joe is shouting and stopping the lorry.
I fall out of my coat into the road.
I don't want to be in Kosovo.
Let me out, let me out, let me out!
(*She falls to her knees, crying and sobbing*)

Hannah   I was thrown out of my corner into the darkness.
The toilet bucket spilt over.
I was wet through.
I can't stand it anymore.
Let me out, let me out, let me out! (*She falls to her knees*)

Hannah ⎫
Hanna ⎬ (*together*) *Let me out, let me out!*

Hannah   The big doors open and there's Joe.

(*As Joe*) Hannah! What the fuck are you doing here?

(*As herself*) Oh Joe, I'm seeking asylum from Margate.

Hannah ⎫
Hanna ⎬ (*together*) And there was Hanna(h).

A lyrical Kosovan folk melody plays, very loud

Hannah and Hanna go mental and jump around the stage together in delight, shouting out each other's name

The music decreases in volume. The girls eventually fall silent and embrace

Hannah   We washed in a river.
              I stuffed my face with food.
              Hanna lent me a clean top.

Hanna gives Hannah the top from around her waist; Hannah puts it on

Hanna   I was ready to jump,
              But Hannah is here.
              I am in Kosovo,
              But Hannah is here.
              I cannot believe it.
              I cannot believe it.

Hannah and Hanna change the US *picture to one of the Kosovan landscape, then sit on the* DS *box and fall asleep*

The Kosovan music continues to play. They wake

SCENE 3

The Lights change to a general state over the whole stage

Hannah and Hanna stand C, *Hanna behind Hannah*

The music fades

Hannah   We woke up.
              I think we woke up anyway.
              Everything seemed slower and brighter.
              I don't remember how we were standing
              By the side of the road
              And no longer in the lorry …
              That's where we were.
              It was getting dark.
              Hanna and me were staring at a coach.
Hanna   That's the coach.
Hannah   A dead coach, you could say.
              It was all brown and black;

Brown with rust and black from fire,
Parked by itself on this empty road.
Mountains all around.
All of a sudden,
Albin goes totally mental.
He runs at the coach,
Pounding the side of it with his feet and his fists,
Bellowing and howling,
And smashing up what's already smashed.

Hanna   We left for Macedonia in that coach;
It was our escape from Kosovo,
The beginning of our journey to Margate.
We were stopped by the Serbs.
They were selecting young people;
Albin and I were both chosen.
My mother was still in that coach.
They would not let her off.
The men were taken off first.
The women were taken to a garage
Twenty minutes down the road,
A big empty building.
The soldiers all had knives and guns;
All were wearing masks.
My clothes were torn off me.
(*She stops*)
At some point the screaming around me stopped;
I think the soldiers got some sort of order.
I do not know why they set us free.
We were taken out of the garage, back to the roadside.
We smelt the coach burning before we saw it.
We met up again with the men.
Albin was there and though he was beaten
He was standing.
He was alive.
I was ashamed for him to see me like this,
But he saw I was alive too.
Not all of the men were there.
The coach was still in flames.
The Serbs made us walk to Macedonia.
I did not know if my mother was dead in the coach.
When I got to the camp in Macedonia I was very bad.
My mother was waiting for us.
She was alive.

She looked after us.
She helped me not to be ashamed.
I cried for weeks and my mother said:
"Don't stop, cry more."
And hugged me.
When Albin told me about a lorry going to England
He said it was the first time that I smiled again.
We could go to England.
Sorry to make you sad.

Hannah says nothing

Say something.

Hannah says nothing

Haven't you got a tongue in your head?
Hannah I'd want to kill the people who did that to me.
Hanna That's what Albin wants to do.
That's why he's come back.
But I do not want that.
Hannah I feel useless.
Hanna You're not.
You're here.
Hannah I called you scum.
Hanna I fought back.
Hannah I feel sick.
I wish I was in Margate.
Hanna So do I.
So much.
Hannah Come back.
I'm not frightened any more
And neither should you be.
They can call us what names they bloody like.
Right?
Hanna Right …
Hannah I know,
We'll sing.
Sing together.
Become a group.
Get on *Top of the Pops* or something — right?
Hanna Right. I can't come.
Hannah Nan'll put you up.

Hanna   I'm not allowed back.
Hannah   Sez who?
Hanna   Once you leave you can't go back. Only if I've got lots of money.
              Or if I marry an English guy ...
Hannah   Marry Joe ...

They laugh

Hannah   Look.
              If you can't come to Margate,
              I'll stay here with you for a while.
              Nan can manage by herself for a bit.
              Wha'd'ya say?
Hanna   Did you bring your passport?
Hannah   Passport?
              No.
              I ain't got one.
              I ain't never bin abroad before.

Hanna drops her head

              I'm sorry about what you told me.
              I'm sorry it happened to you.
              I'm sorry.
Hanna   Why haven't you got a passport?
              Then you could stay for a bit.
              I wish I had a British passport.
              I could live in Margate.
              I wouldn't have to be here in Kosovo
              And live with people who want to kill each other.
              You don't see Margate like me.
              It's a beautiful town.
              One day other people will go there
              And they will see it too.
              (*Pointing*) Look,
              Mother and Albin are waiting for me.
              Joe is waiting for you.
              He still has to deliver the medicines before he takes you home.
              Just a mile up that little road is where we sleep tonight
              Before we go to Pristina;
              From here we walk.

Hannah turns and faces Hanna

Hannah Is this it?
Hanna   Yes.
            This is it.

Hannah and Hanna sing "Torn", unaccompanied. They have a new sound, more experimental, not gloomy, a mixture of pop and folk

Hannah and Hanna exit separately

Black-out

FURNITURE AND PROPERTY LIST

ACT I

On stage: Picture signifying Margate with narrow ledge below it
Two wooden boxes about the size of an average suitcase — side by side
us forming a platform. *On one*: operational karaoke machine
Two screens. *Behind* **Hannah***'s*: Aldi's overall, chair, laundry bag,
pile of library books, newspaper. *Behind* **Hanna***'s*: supermarket
basket and shopping voucher, different-style chair, handbag
Pier railings. *Hanging from them*: two identical baseball caps

Off stage: Photographs (**Hannah** and **Hanna**)

Personal: **Hanna**: bandanna

ACT II

Set: Picture of grey sea with seagulls (Margate and Kosovo pictures ready
behind it)
Boxes on sides with gap between them. *In* **Hannah***'s box*: Walkman
headphones, two letters, 2000 headband. *In* **Hanna***'s box*: Walkman
headphones, party popper, two letters, long-sleeved top

Strike: Railings
Chairs

Off stage: Rucksack (**Hannah**)

LIGHTING PLOT

Practical fittings required: nil
Various interiors and exteriors on a bare stage

ACT I

To open: General lighting

Cue 1	**Hannah**: "On a hot summer night." *Change to setting evoking seafront by night*	(Page 3)
Cue 2	**Hanna**: "I didn't mean to take her name." *Change to different outdoor setting*	(Page 4)
Cue 3	**Hannah** stands behind the counter *Change to indoor setting*	(Page 6)
Cue 4	**Hanna** and **Hannah** knock over the boxes and exit *Change to setting evoking seafront by night*	(Page 7)
Cue 5	**Hanna** runs her fingers along the railings *Change to indoor setting*	(Page 8)
Cue 6	**Hannah** comes out with laundry bag, books, newspaper *Change to different indoor setting*	(Page 9)
Cue 7	**Hannah**: "Magnetic, see?" *Change to outdoor setting*	(Page 11)
Cue 8	"By the River" plays *Change to different outdoor setting*	(Page 15)
Cue 9	**Hannah**: "I was shaking." *Change to indoor setting*	(Page 15)

ACT II

To open: Darkness

Cue 10	When ready *Bring up general exterior lighting*	(Page 21)

EFFECTS PLOT

ACT I

Cue 1   **Hannah** switches on the karaoke machine   (Page 3)
"I Should Be So Lucky" from machine

Cue 2   **Hannah** switches off the tape   (Page 3)
Cut "I Should Be So Lucky" but keep microphone operational

Cue 3   **Hannah** switches on the karaoke machine   (Page 7)
"Baby One More Time" from machine

Cue 4   **Hannah** switches off the tape   (Page 8)
Cut "Baby One More Time"

Cue 5   **Hannah**: "Course I'll be there."   (Page 11)
"Right Here Right Now" over theatre speakers

Cue 6   **Hannah**: "Magnetic, see?"   (Page 11)
Increase volume of music; play to end of song

Cue 7   **Hannah**: " … grit your teeth, don't you?"   (Page 15)
"By the River" over theatre speakers

Cue 8   **Hannah**: "And slams the door."   (Page 16)
Cut "By the River"

Cue 9   **Hannah**: "At the time. Right?"   (Page 18)
"Torn" over theatre speakers

Cue 10   **Hanna**: "I want to be a pharmacist."   (Page 19)
Fade "Torn"

ACT II

Cue 11   **Hannah**: " …me they wanted to hurt, not Hanna."   (Page 21)
Piano version of "Good King Wenceslas"
over theatre speakers

Cue 12   Choreographed sequence ends   (Page 21)
"Good King Wenceslas" ends

Cue 13   **Hannah**: " … grey shite and seagulls."   (Page 22)
            Piano version of "Little Girl Blue" over theatre speakers

Cue 14   **Hannah** and **Hanna** sing "Little Girl Blue" to the end   (Page 22)
            Fade music

Cue 15   **Hannah**: " … like it as much as I do."   (Page 24)
            A-Teens' "Mamma Mia" over theatre speakers

Cue 16   **Hannah/Hannah**: "January. February. March. April."   (Page 24)
            Increase volume of music

Cue 17   **Hannah** and **Hanna** dance   (Page 24)
            Decrease volume of music

Cue 18   **Hanna** changes the picture and moves the boxes   (Page 25)
            Bring up volume of music for finale

Cue 19   **Hannah**: "I was gone."   (Page 27)
            *"Are You Better Off Alone" loudly, then quietly
              over theatre speakers*

Cue 20   **Hanna**: "Hannah!"   (Page 28)
            Increase volume of music

Cue 21   **Hannah** and **Hanna** change the Margate picture   (Page 28)
            Cut music abruptly

Cue 22   **Hannah/Hanna**: "And there was Hanna(h)."   (Page 31)
            Lyrical Kosovan folk melody, very loud

Cue 23   **Hannah** and **Hanna** jump around the stage   (Page 32)
            Decrease volume of music

Cue 24   **Hannah** and **Hanna** stand c   (Page 32)
            Fade music

A licence issued by Samuel French Ltd to perform this play does not include permission to use the Incidental music specified in this copy. Where the place of performance is already licensed by the PERFORMING RIGHT SOCIETY a return of the music used must be made to them. If the place of performance is not so licensed then application should be made to the PERFORMING RIGHT SOCIETY, 29-33 Berners Street, London W1T 4AB.

A separate and additional licence from PHONOGRAPHIC PERFORMANCES LTD, Ganton House, 1 Upper James Street, London W1R 3HG is needed whenever commercial recordings are used.